Contents

Detailed Walks

1. **By V...**   2
   Queb...
2. **Bana...**   4
   Queb...
3. **Socorridos Valley.**   6
   Santa Quiteria 1.5hrs 5km.
4. **Another Way Home.**   8
   Santa Quiteria-Funchal 1.5hrs 5km.

Link Walk 4A.   11
Linking Walk 4 to Walk 1 0.5hrs 2 km.

5. **The Pilgrim's Stair.**   12
   Terreiro da Luta-Monte 1hr 3km.
6. **Spa to Refuge.**   14
   Monte-Romeiros 1hr 3km.
7. **Tornos-Jasmin Tea House.**   16
   Romeiros-Palheiro Ferreiro 2hrs 7km.
8. **Da Serra West.**   19
   Valle do Paraiso-Foguete 2hrs 6km.
9. **Da Serra East.**   22
   Vale do Pariaso-Camacha 2hrs 7km.
10. **A Little Bit of Everything.**   25
    Foguete-Jardim Botanico 1hr 3km.
11. **Camacha to Jasmin Tea House.**   27
    Camacha-Palheiro Ferreiro 2hrs 6 kilometres.
12. **Levada do Caniçal (West).**   28
    Maroços-Tunel do Caniçal 3hrs 12km.
13. **A Peak Effort.**   30
    Machico-Pico do Facho-Caniçal 2hrs 7km.
14. **Levada do Caniçal (East).**   33
    Tunel do Caniçal-Canical 1.5hrs 5.5km.
15. **All-Weather Strolling.**   35
    Machico-Ribeira Seca-Machico 2hrs 7.5km.
16. **Boca do Risco.**   37
    Ribeira Seca-Boca do Risco 2hrs 7km.
17. **Descent from Portela.**   39
    Portela-Maroços 1hr 4km.
18. **The Quiet Forest.**   40
    Faja dos Rolos circular 3hrs 11km.

Hillside Picnic.   42

Glossary   43
Index   44

1

1. BY WATERWAY TO FUNCHAL.

Our most easily accessible country walk. If your hotel is on the main tourist road, Estrada Monumental, then catch the N°2 bus outside your hotel and our "step by step" guide will bring you back to the foyer. You can walk the route in reverse, but it is a steep (1 in 3 in places) 100 metre ascent to the levada. We follow the Levada dos Piornais from its appearance at Quebradas, through a surprising mixture of town and countryside, into the outskirts of Funchal, and then we skitter down a flower-lined lane and road to finish back at our hotel.

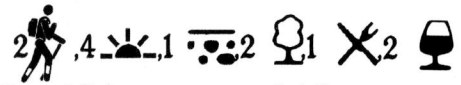

2 🚶, 4 ☀ 1 🍽 2 🌳 1 ✕ 2 🍷

Time 1.5 hours, approx 6 kilometres.
Ascents 0 metres, descents 90 metres.

Jump on a N°2 bus (heading out of town) and unless the driver does something very unusual he will pull up under the motorway bridge fifteen minutes later at the terminus in Quebradas. From the bus, we are only a few metres from the start of "Funchal's Waterway", but as you may not see Quebradas again, why not take a short stroll around "Banana Valley" and enjoy the hospitality at Bar Santa Rita (see Walk 2) before heading back to town. From the N°2 terminus we walk back along the bus route for 20 metres and turn right down a tarmac road to find a levada sign "L.V.", and an arrow pointing down some steps. At N°393 we find the levada. Our route is along the levada wall, a well surfaced path approximately 0.5 metres wide. On these walls you must concentrate on where you put your feet, "Stop to look at the views". Two hundred metres on we find the levada paved over to become a wide walkway. We pass bananas and a pair of new houses below us before reaching a new house built on the levada. Taking the steps alongside the house, we come to a cobbled roadway which we follow up to the main road. Crossing the road, we head down past garage doors to rejoin the paved levada walkway. We follow the path as it curves around a barren knoll with a bleak glass-block wall on our right. Wild flowers on the hillside alleviate this rather bleak section of our route. As the wall ends, so does the paving, and we are back onto a levada wall (take care). We have views over Funchal's outskirts beyond the hotel area, while above us are examples of cochineal beetle living on the prickly pear. After a few hundred metres the wild area gives way to grape vine-fenced banana plots as our route runs around this valley

Walk 1 By Waterway to Funchal

pocket between occasional houses. At the apex of the pocket we pass a sluice gate section of the levada. The front gate of House 294 opens onto our route, and the quality of the wall improves. We continue, overlooking new housing developments, until we cross a cobbled street and houses now line the levada as we meet a low bridge which we skirt around. Back on the levada we curve left passing banana plots below us and stairs accessing the higher slopes coming down to meet the levada route. Past a disused water tank, we enter a former cultivated area which has now run wild. We pass above a shanty and come onto a dirt path which gives a welcome rest from the "wall". For a hundred metres there is a bit of a drop on our right before we come to some corrugated iron cladding. If you are worried about crossing this section, follow our tip; walk with one foot each side of the levada - it looks ungainly but it works. Past the cladding, the path is very easy, as we pass a hillside of blue tajinastes. The levada disappears, and for a few metres we walk above it on a dirt path before rejoining the waterway. After house N°228 we have a short slabbed section before we are back on the wall. Just on the corner we see the turret chimney of an old house (N°243) followed by another old house, before we come to a communal washing area, still in use. Here at the local "twin-tub" people come to beat their clothes into submission at the shallow basins fed from the levada. Back onto the levada's uneven wall, we come to a catchment grill and we can see civilisation straight ahead in the form of an electricity substation, as we come to a tarmac road. Geraniums mask our temporary departure from the levada, as we head up a concrete drive onto the road. Across the road to the parking area, and at N°16 there is a small shop and bar behind the green doors, conveniently placed for taking a refreshment break.

From the bar we walk along the paved levada into the Amparo area and in 20 metres we are back on the cobbled levada wall passing between houses. Back onto paving and back on the wall, we head towards a small cobbled road crossing the levada. As we follow the contour around the hill and past a new house, the vista below us opens out. We are now looking over new apartment blocks down to the sea. Passing new houses and gardens, we come to steps down from the levada, just before a breeze-block wall. After the wall there is an area where agave americana plants have established themselves on the abandoned slope below us. A few minutes on we pass a grill in the levada, and come onto

Walk 1 By Waterway to Funchal

loose laid slabs which produce a comforting "boing" as we walk on them. As we approach some new houses the ground drops away from the wall, and we recommend using the path on the left of the waterway until reaching the houses. We walk past the roof level of these dwellings and head on towards a new apartment complex. Below us is an excellent view down over the hotel area and Rock "Pimple". With the hotels below us we come to house N°102, above us, from where the levada is paved over. We pass the apartments at their fourth floor level before turning round the hillside to a level change in the levada. Steps take us past the level change and over a bridge to pass between houses 70 and 87 to meet the levada again. For a short stretch our route is hemmed in by banana plots and house walls until the paving ends and we are again walking along the wall. On this last stretch we turn around the hill to look over the main area of Funchal and the port, as we pass house N°17. Our finish is only a few minutes away, as we pass small houses and cultivated plots, with villas above us, and turn right to head for a wide tarmac road. Straight across the road, down the steps, and we are back on the levada wall. We pass a concrete stair coming down from the road above, and continue to the next set of stairs where we walk up to the road. On the road, we are just past a bus stop and we could catch a N°45 for a lengthy ride back to our hotel. However, as it is all downhill we will walk along towards the back of the stadium. At the pink house we turn right and follow Ladeira de Casa Brava which heads steeply downhill past Quinta das Voltas and is lined with an excellent variety of flowers. Half a kilometre down, we drop onto Rua da Casa Branca by house N°20A and turn right. Rua da Casa Branca snakes downhill to meet the main road alongside the Monumental Lido Hotel, and opposite the Eden Mar.

2. BANANARAMA.

Having arrived at Quebradas on the N°2 bus, it would be a waste not to complete this short levada walk in "Banana Valley" before starting our "By Waterway to Funchal" levada route into town. Although this walk takes only an hour, it is a good example of how communities were built around levada access routes before the car became dominant.

Walk 2 Bananarama.

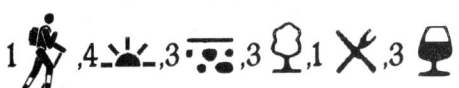

1 🚶 ,4 ☀️ ,3 🍽️ ,3 🌳 ,1 🍴 ,3 🍷

Time 1 hour, approx 3 kilometres.
Ascents & descents negligible.

We start at the N°2 bus terminus as for Walk 1, but this time we walk in the opposite direction up to the T-junction. A "Levada dos Piornais" sign by house N°32 points left, and we turn down the main road, passing a supermarket/bar and on our right on top of a tall pole is a sign to Bar/Super Santa Rita - our refreshment stop at the end of the walk. Past the school, and a road bridge over the motorway, we come to a public water tap and ahead is a sign, "Levada dos Piornais" pointing right, where we find the levada in the apex of a sharp right bend in the road, just past house N°62. Up the steps from the road, and we come onto the wide concrete flagged roof of the levada heading into "Banana Valley". A few metres on and we pass above the first house, Casa 66, we follow the tall wall on our right into the valley. Behind us the roads drops down to Lombada, and behind that the motorway "flies" across the gorge on its impressive bridge over the Socorridos Valley. Set into the wall are entrance doorways to the houses out of sight above us, numbers 356 and 358. We soon leave the traffic noise behind us as our route takes us around this sea of bananas. Below us, new houses are dotted among the plantations along with older traditional dwellings. The wall on our right drops to eye level and now the bananas, fenced by gnarled grape vines, are above us as well as below us. It is easy walking on the wide paved levada, as we enter a small corner of the valley to find a pocket of terraced houses split by a small, steep ravine. A few of the concrete flags are missing from the levada cover, and as their wooden replacements look none too reassuring, watch where you walk on this section. We pass a long stair of concrete steps just by house 410, before the levada passes under a cobbled road which heads further inland. Our levada path turns back towards the sea, leaving the upper plantations, and villas on an outcrop overlooking the valley, behind us. Down a couple of steps, and we continue on the levada path. Our contour line route runs along the west side of the valley to cross a concrete roadway running down to gates onto a cobbled road. Above us is house 464, just before the path comes into open views across the valley to our start point. As we approach the valley's mouth, the banana floor drops away, and we head for the

Walk 2 Bananarama.

motorway bridge. House 494 marks the levada's turn to the right towards main gorge of the Socorridos valley. Cages of birds on the terrace of 506 (a blue and white house) sing our turn out of the small valley. As we parallel the motorway, houses now line the slope above the levada. We come to 526 to cross a cobbled track and climb up onto a platform above a levada level change, to look across the Socorridos valley. Flying across the gorge with its art-deco "arrow-heads", the motorway leaps this formidable obstacle. Impressive cliff walls box in the valley as it slopes to the sea. You can continue beyond the level change, preferably if you have four legs with a cloven hoof on the end of each, but it does mean walking on the levada wall above a sheer drop, or scrambling around the hillside. For us, we will stroll back by the same route, and by the time we are sitting on Bar Santa Rita's terrace, we will be able to discuss banana cultivation like experts!

3. SOCORRIDOS VALLEY.

The Socorridos Valley was once one of the most exciting, vertigo prone, walks of southern Madeira, with unforgettable views over the massive canyon. In recent times rockfalls have made the levada extremely dangerous, although the water continues to flow, resulting in the island government signing the route as "impassable", just where the levada starts its run along the canyon wall. While the most spectacular views are no longer accessible, this still makes a pleasant country walk to the edge of the "Grand Canyon" and back.

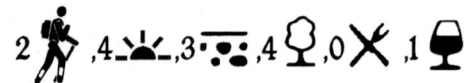

Time 1.5 hours, approx 5 kilometres.
Ascents 50 metres, descents 50 metres.

We start by catching the bus (8 or 16) and staying on board until it reaches its terminus at Santa Quintera. From the bus, we walk uphill in front of house numbers 59 and 61, with a factory on our right and passing a small bar on the left. Just past the bar we look for a narrow alley leading down from the road just after N°65. We head down the alley passing houses on our right, until after 200 metres the path drops down some steps onto a tarmac road. Following the road, we head steeply downhill past a banana plantation before we

Walk 3 Socorridos Valley

turn left, and then bend right to find the paved levada leading away from Funchal - the start of Walk 4, "Another Way Home". We continue for a few metres past two houses on our left, to find the open levada at the end of a parking area. Leaving the tarmac behind, we walk carefully along the levada wall. Shortly, a stone path crosses the waterway, giving us a view down through the ranks of bananas to the sea. We begin to pass houses built alongside the levada; a blue house followed by N°127, whose access is the narrow wall that we are walking on. Turning a corner, we come out to views down the valley, and a stone path drops steeply down from our route as some new houses come into view. The levada leads us into the valley pocket containing the new houses, and we meet the first of the access paths coming down to the waterway. After the narrow wall we come to a stretch of paving covering the levada, allowing for more relaxed walking. Past new house N°145, we are now strolling between banana plantations until we emerge to look down a steep stone path into the valley. As we steadily turn around the hillside we pass above a communal washing area and our route crosses a water level change to come to a stone road leading down from the town. Beyond the road we are back onto the levada wall. We pass above a banana plot before coming out into an open landscape covered in a profusion of wild flowers on both sides of the levada.

We have now turned into the small valley through which the Ribeira do Arvoredo runs. Our narrow wall runs past a house with a colourful garden, N°7, to meet a concrete road coming down from Santa Quintera. From the roadway the levada forms an important access way for the houses further up the valley, and has been paved. This wide walkway is quite a relief after so much walking on the narrow levada wall. Looking across the valley, we can see our route emerge from the valley above the small green house directly opposite us. A rock cliff stands above our route, while down in the valley the gaunt shapes of tall, dead trees stand out like silver-grey fingers against the verdant background. After the last house we come into a country meadow landscape as we head for a stand of eucalyptus trees while down below us are the polished grey boulders marking the route of the river along the valley floor. As we approach the eucalyptus trees we find a last, isolated house above the levada. Leaving the meadow behind, we are in a wood where the eucalyptus trees soar fifty metres above us, and stretch as far up the hillside as we can see. The wood is light and airy, as we stroll through it to

Walk 3 Socorridos Valley.

a bridge over the river. At the bridge, complete with levada, there is a distinct change of scene. Across the ravine is an incomplete house overhung with dank foliage. As we cross the wooden planked bridge we come under a dark, dripping cliff wall. Be careful on this section, as the drops of water have worn away complete sections of the paving slabs, just leaving the reinforcing rods hanging on. A handrail lines the route as the valley floor drops away below us. The dripping cliff is soon passed, and the guard rail finishes as we come into an area of cultivated plots. We pass the first house this side of the valley, N°19. More houses and then we meet access steps going up from the levada to Caminho Dos Tres Paus Aviana. A couple more minutes and we are passing the green house and steps down signed "Entrada N°41". Levada do Curral now turns sharply away from the valley of Ribeira do Arvoredo, rounding a slope covered with viper's bugloss, to enter the canyon that is the Socorridos Valley. Past a water level change and we continue above houses into the valley, its true magnificence hidden from us by a stand of bamboo and eucalyptus. Clear of the trees, we come to an open space. There in front of us is the Socorridos Valley - in front, below and across from us. Terraces reach down from the top levels to the bottom of the canyon, almost all of them in cultivation. The paving finishes here and we take to the levada wall for the last few metres round the cliff to the sign closing the levada for safety reasons. From this point we have superb views of this great canyon, and can only marvel at the experiences enjoyed by earlier walkers who could progress beyond this point, on the exciting but VERY vertiginous levada. For us it is a gentle stroll back to our start point, and a decision on how to return to town.

4. ANOTHER WAY HOME.

From the end (and start) of Walk 3 "Socorridos Valley", we eschew the bus and walk back into town along the Levada do Curral until it disappears. A pleasing mixture of cultivated plots, countryside and village can be enjoyed before we join the last stage of Walk 1 for a descent back to the hotel. After approx. 2.5 kilometres, there is a Link Walk, 4A, down to Levada dos Piornais.

Walk 4 Another Way Home.

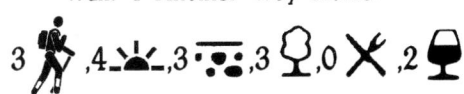

3 🚶 ,4 ⛰ ,3 🍽 ,3 🍷 ,0 ✕ ,2 🍸

Time 1.5 hours, approx 5 kilometres.
Ascents negligible, descents 250 metres.

We arrive at Santa Quintera and follow the start of Walk 3, to arrive at the Levada do Curral. As we come down to the houses, a concrete path slopes down onto the paved levada leading off to our left. We follow the levada round below a stone wall, passing above N°107, Vivenda Grascinda, to come into overgrown countryside where the paving finishes, so that we continue on the narrow levada wall. We head into the pocket of the valley to cross a water runoff at the head of the pocket. Wild flowers cover the walls and the abandoned terraces below us, as we come to a level change in the levada and emerge from the valley onto a tarmac street. Here paths lead off both up and down the slopes as we follow the levada along the street past N°91. Five minutes along the street it turns in front of the Soares da Costa factory which marks the start of a mixture of new and old housing as the road drops a metre below the level of the levada. As the street narrows between older houses, the levada disappears into a tunnel and we come to a cross-roads.

Across from us is the sign "Caminho do Pico do Funcho", while just to our right are the green doors (N.77) of an unnamed local bar. The levada has completely disappeared at this point, so we head across the junction and follow Caminho do Pico do Funcho round to Bar Mariano. As we approach the bar there is a small alley signed "Levada do Pico do Funcho" off to our right, but we continue on past (or to) the bar, to find the levada below a sign, "Parada de Levada do Poço Barral". We leave the street and go onto the levada, passing through a banana plantation. A stone stairway joins the levada from our left, just before we turn a corner to pass a second stairway. We pass behind a bottling plant to cross a concrete path running down the hillside and continue on the "paved" levada. We pass through an area of cottages in a multitude of styles to cross a second concrete path and pass a community building with three sets of green doors, to come into more open countryside on our left as we continue along the paved levada. Houses bunch together on the right as our route becomes a narrow alley, notable for the tiling on house N°4, before we pop out onto a main road at a pedestrian crossing alongside a local bar, N°33B.

Walk 4 Another Way Home.

We head down the road towards São Martinho church. Fifty metres down the road, we come to a modern bar on our left and a road signed, "Travesa do Moyno". From this point Link Walk 4A would take us down to São Martinho church. Turning left onto Travesa do Mayno, we find that the levada emerges just around the corner. We pass villa N°6 and follow the levada on a small path alongside bananas. At the corner of the bananas the levada comes to a level change and runs steeply downhill. We take the steps down past house N°1 where the levada is diverted into a modern aqueduct supported on concrete pillars. We go along to a pedestrian bridge and climb up over the Via Rapida. The bridge takes us above the motorway to pass behind a military compound onto a wide path running alongside the levada, which resumes its pre-motorway route at this point. Below us houses are set down amongst the bananas as our route curves round the hillside towards Funchal. The views change from villas and mountains to apartment blocks and Funchal harbour as we follow the levada. Suddenly the levada turns downhill and plunges into a culvert. We follow the raging torrent on a steep stairway to emerge outside house N°33 onto a road access. The levada turns right to continue on a contour line, before dropping down at house N°29 to follow the road. We follow the waterway on cobbled and concrete steps until we come back onto the tarmac outside the entrance to N°13A. The levada continues as a channel by the side of the road. We follow it down past housing and down an alley where we emerge onto Rua Dr. Bareto outside the green doors of N°7. This is the last we see of the levada as it disappears underground, and for us it is now all downhill to the hotel. We walk along Rua Dr. Bareto to its junction with the main road. Taking extreme care, we cross straight over this busy road to the Caminho do Avista Navios. The caminho runs gently uphill for a short stretch before settling into its downhill run. We pass the entrance to Quinta do Avista Navios, followed shortly by the Quinta da Bela Vista (now a five star hotel). At the end of Quinta da Bela Vista we continue downhill on the Rua da Africa do Sul, which soon becomes the Caminho da Nazaré. On our left is a water tap (working), just before we start passing the apartment blocks of the Nazaré area on our right and a walkway down to the Rua do Dr. Pita on our left. We stay on the road and head down to a right angled bend. On the corner, a dirt footpath goes across open ground, and on the first lamp-post we find a sign, "Caminho da Nazaré", with arrows pointing

Walk 4 Another Way Home.

both ways. We come onto an old stone-laid path cutting across the open ground behind the schools. Passing a house on our right, we drop down some concrete steps onto a tarmac access road, still the Caminho da Nazaré. Our route runs down over a cobbled area, following the road steeply downhill until we emerge onto the road running around the back of the stadium. Crossing carefully over the road, we come to the Ladeira da Casa Branca, running steeply downhill. On our right are the green painted handrails at the end of the Levada dos Piornais (Walk 1). From here we follow the Ladeira steeply downhill to Rua da Casa Branca, and to the hotel area on the same finishing route as Walk 1.

LINK WALK 4A (Walk 4 to Walk1).

Levada dos Piornais (Walks 1 & 2) at 150 metres, and Levada do Curral (Walks 3 & 4) at 270 metres altitude, run on almost parallel routes as they approach Funchal, and our walks have a common finishing point at the rear of the stadium to descend back to the hotel area. This link walk joins routes 4 and 1 at approximately the mid-point of the levada section of each walk. On Walk 4 where we emerge onto a main road by a pedestrian crossing, we continue down the main road to São Martinho church, instead of continuing on Levada do Curral. We come down to the square below the church. Above the square is a garden bar for refreshments before we head down the road away from Funchal. Half a kilometre down from the square, stairs lead off to the left of the road. Follow the stairs down and turn left on the concrete path as it runs along the valley wall. The path slopes down to run between houses and emerge on an access road. We pass the pasteleria Dona Xepa and the road climbs gently. Front right we can see the electricity substation where we will join Walk 1 on the Levada dos Piornais. A kilometre along the lane finds us climbing up to meet a road. We turn right to head downhill and shortly come to a main road and the sign "Camaro do Amparo" pointing back the way we have come. From the bar on the corner of Camara do Amparo we head steeply downhill to the electricity substation. At the point where the Levada dos Piornais passes under the road, we have a choice. Right, past the electricity substation, would take us along the levada for a short walk into Quebradas. Left, in front of the bar, is a slightly longer route into the outskirts of Funchal and a skitter down from behind the stadium to the hotel area.

5. THE PILGRIM'S STAIR.

Take an impressive monument and view (if it's not cloudy), add an historical religious route (which hardly anyone knows about) and a finish with refreshments in a former health spa, and you have our "Pilgrim's Stair". It is all downhill; sometimes very downhill, and can be tough on the calves and knees so although this is a short walk, take rests when you feel it is necessary. Unfortunately since our first edition the monument has been enclosed by a fence and the massive chains have been removed along with the NESW fountain; such is the price of progress!

3 🚶 ,4 ☀ ,3 ☕ ,4 🌳 ,1 ✕ ,3 🍸

Time 1 hour, approx 3 kilometres.
Ascents nil, descents 300 metres.

We reach the Terreiro da Luta by taking the N°48 Nazaré-Monte bus from the hotel area, or 20 or 21 buses from Avenida do Mar, to arrive at our finish point, and then take a taxi up to the monument. Your taxi driver will drop you at the largest statue on Madeira, the "Lady of Peace". We walk back along the road towards the junction of the E-201 and the E-103 towards Quinta da Luta to find a traditional pebble path down below us. Going down the broad cobbled path, we start down the "Pilgrim's Stair". Alongside is a gurgling water channel, as we turn down around the garden of the quinta. Down the wide stair-effect cobbled path, we drop rapidly towards Monte. Alongside our route the pines and eucalyptus trees blend their invigorating fragrances, adding a spring to our downward steps. To our right, through the trees, we catch glimpses down the valley over Monte to Funchal in the distance. Our steep descent is interrupted by a woodland glen where a spring joins the small levada. Looking back through the flowering mimosas, we can still catch glimpses of the Da Luta hermitage high above us. From the glen, we resume our descent on the cobbled stair, pines on our right and mimosas on our left. The stair heads relentlessly down (but even more relentlessly up if you walk this route in reverse) with occasional twists and turns as it descends this steep pocket of the valley. As we descend, the pines on our right thin out to give the walk an airy feel, along with views across the valley. We come to a section where the stair descends in a series of zigzags, the tiny levada piped under the turns. As we pass a plane tree on our right we come to a gap in the woodland, to look down on a

Walk 5 The Pilgrim's Stair.

classic quinta with a round observatory tower. Here the path starts to approach the outskirts of Monte. Finally, a steep downhill section brings us out of the forest to the first house. The path becomes tarmac strips as it passes the house, to meet a cobbled road as the fast-flowing mini levada plunges into a culvert.

Standing on the cobbled road, with views down over Funchal, we have a choice of ways. Dropping away to our right, the cobbled road is a simple route down into Monte, but we will take the old footpaths for our finish. We take the stone path going down to our left, past a sign "Vereda das Quintas". It is straight downhill between cottages and vegetable plots, before the path starts to snake between the old houses as it gently descends. We come down in a series of little zigzags to a concrete path running off to our right, signed "Beco da Pereira", just in front of house N°28. Continuing on the stone path, we pass N°26, one of the few new houses in this area, to come to a junction of paths and a working public water tap. Across on our right is the quinta we saw earlier, and a concrete path, while we continue down left on the stone "staired" pathway. The path drops steeply between houses and vegetable plots as it snakes down the hillside. "Vereda das Quintas", a stone walkway heading off to our left, provides access to houses round the hill, as we continue steeply down towards the centre of Monte. On our left is an old quinta wall with an ivy covered archway, opposite house N°11. After the old wall we drop straight down for a hundred metres between a black boulder wall on our left and a concrete wall on our right. The "stair" effect stone path is supplemented by concrete stairs, as we pass houses on our right. At the end of this straight section our path turns in front of a bricked-up entry, and becomes a road access. To our left a dirt road curves away behind the wall that we have been following. We follow the tarmac strips down to meet a cobbled road and a sign "Caminho das Laginhas", pointing back the way we have come. We walk down the cobbled road to a parking area with a road sign "Caminho das Tilias" pointing away to our right. Across the road is a small viewing area with green railings, from which we look down onto the central square and ornamental gardens of Monte. From here, we could follow the road right or go down the concrete stairs from the viewing point. We take the "traditional" Vereda da Fonte route down the stairs, onto a stone path heading steeply downhill into the gardens above the square. We have a choice of stone-laid paths down into

Walk 5 The Pilgrim's Stair.

the square and can take refreshment at the Cafe do Parque (popular with tourists), or Gregorio's unnamed bar just up from the bandstand (local prices), in this picturesque setting.

6. SPA TO REFUGE.

Combining an historic health resort, Madeira's sledge run, ornamental gardens, cobbled roads and old stone-laid walkways passing through some excellent countryside, this route is one of our short-walk favouries. There is a small price to pay as we descend into a steep valley and have to ascend the other side - a stiff climb compared to some levada walks. We start at the former health resort of Monte which we reach direct from Funchal's hotel area on the N°48 bus (weekdays only) or from Avenida do Mar on the 20 or 21 services.

This route can be walked in reverse, bus N°29 to Romeiros, or as an extension of Walk 7 in reverse. The final stage into Babosas is a steep, unrelenting climb followed by a stroll into Monte for refreshments in the square.

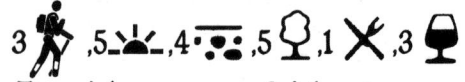

3 ,.5 ,.4 ,.5 ,.1 ,.3

Time 1 hour, approx 3 kilometres.
Ascents 120 metres, descents 120 metres.

We start by walking a few metres up from the bus terminus onto the pebbled roads and pavements of Monte's square. Taking a break beneath the magnificent plane trees it is easy to see how Monte became a fashionable health spa in the early twentieth century. Our route starts from the bandstand following the path signed to "Babosas" round the landscaped hillside below Monte's famous church, Nossa Sênhora do Monte. We are on a one-way cobbled road (open to traffic) curving left to come around to the 68 steps leading up to the church. Opposite the stairway is a viewing point overlooking the "push off" point of Monte's sleigh run, the "Carros do Cesto" slide down to the upper reaches of Funchal. We drop down behind the start of the sled run to follow the cobbled road away from Monte. Watching out for traffic we curve left to overlook the Japanese style ornamental gardens. At the garden's entry point the road turns right for us to walk gently up past the "Old Monte Tavern" and "Old Monte

Walk 6 Spa to Refuge.

Gardens" before the road swings left to come down into the square in front of Babosas' unusual twin-belfry church.

Across the square is a mirador overlooking the magnificent Ribeira do João Gomes valley. Tree lined slopes plunge down to the valley floor, and rising up the cliffs facing us with the first of Romeiros' houses visible on the promontory across from us. Following the "Levada dos Tornos" sign we head down the wide stone path from the mirador into the valley. We come steeply down (be careful if the path is wet) under the valley's inland cliff face with a few vegetable terraces below us on our right. Flowering mimosa/acacia trees overhang the route, which is lined with a profusion of wild flowers; viper's bugloss and wild nasturtiums being particularly numerous. We pass a bridge wall, two hundred metres into the descent, carrying a small levada channel. The channel follows a contour line along the valley wall, but its angle when viewed against the path's steep slope creates the illusion that the water is running uphill. Impressive rock cliffs overhang the stone path as our route flattens out above more vegetable plots at a mirador built out from the path; more spectacular views. Round a promontory in the cliff wall and the path drops steeply down with a stair-effect built into its surface; very necessary on this 1 in 3 slope, especially if wet. At the end of the steep descent a well trodden dirt path winds away up towards the head of the valley as we continue down the 'stair' as it zig-zags towards the valley floor. After two zig-zags the path flattens out to run through woodland and turn down to an old bridge. Ten metres below us the water bubbles along under the bridge while above us tree covered cliffs march up the line of the watercourse into the upper valley.

From the bridge we head slowly uphill through the trees on the start of our ascent to Romeiros. Our route is lined with wild flowers and mimosa/acacia trees as we climb up above the valley floor; the path changing to a 'stair-effect' as the gradient increases. Our first 'stair' of a hundred metres takes us up to turn under a white cliff and then we are climbing steeply up through zig-zags. It is a stiff climb relieved by some unusually shaped plane trees contrasting with the straight eucalyptuses in this area. We continue upward accompanied by the pungent aroma of "Naples garlic" which lines a section of the zig-zagging path and past a small cave a faint trail comes to join the stone 'stair' as clear skies above us show that we are approaching the end of our ascent. At last the 'stair' reverts to a gently sloping stone path to

Walk 6 Spa to Refuge.

bring us out of the trees just before we pass below an abandoned house. Looking back our steep descent from Babosas is clearly outlined as it winds down into the valley. Curving left we climb up another 'stair' section past a white cliff and a stone stairway off to our left as we come up to catch glimpses of the outlying houses of Romeiros above us. Our path levels out as we come under the first house and the trees are replaced with alpine-like meadows alongside our route as we pass under a cliff and swing left to come to the start of the village. Passing house N°1 we enter the village to follow the path, now concreted, between the houses. Good examples of intricate chimneys and 'lucky' corner tiles adorn the older house roofs as we pass a water tap and come up to a community building with a flagpole projecting from its first storey. After the flagpole our path runs downhill towards the parking area that is the terminus for the N°29 bus.

If you intend to continue walking along the Levada dos Tornos then take the concrete steps with hand railings just where the cobbled path starts to run downhill. Up the steps and we come onto the paved levada to turn right and taking care not to be caught out by missing slabs and intrusive trees we walk along to come onto a dirt path that meets a cobbled path coming up from the bus terminus. A few metres past this junction is a pale blue building looking like a country railway station, beyond which we find the open levada and its path.

7. TORNOS TO JASMIN TEA HOUSE.

Running along the 600 metre contour line the Levada dos Tornos forms the lower section of south-east Madeira's water distribution system and is a popular walking route for much of its length. This section is close to Funchal and easily accessible while providing a mixture of old and new woodland with villages, a country manor (quinta) and a notable refreshment stop at the Jasmin Tea House. If you have started from Monte on Walk 6 this route provides a straightforward extension to your walking.

Walk 7 Tornos to Jasmin Tea House.
Time 2 hours, approx 7 kilometres.
Ascents/descents negligible.

We start at the Monk's Refuge village of Romeiros on the N°29 bus or after completing Walk 6. We normally start at Romeiros but in wet weather it is advisable to shorten the route by asking the bus driver for the Levada dos Tornos stop and start by climbing up the concrete stair by the bus stop to the levada 1.5km and 35 minutes from Romeiros. The first part of the route from Romeiros runs through some ancient woodland but there are places where the levada has been bridged to protect it from water plunging down the steep ravines when it is raining. In dry weather crossing these bridges is straightforward, but if the torrents are running it becomes extremely hazardous trying to cross the fast flowing water on slippery rock. If you are unfortunate and experience these adverse conditions retrace your steps back to Romeiros and then follow the road to the clearly marked 'levada bus stop' to join the levada at that point.

Alighting from the N°29 bus onto the tarmac parking area we take the concrete steps and cobbled path going steeply up towards the village - do not follow the road. Where the cobbled path flattens out we take the concrete steps on our right to climb up to a 'country railway station' style building standing beside the paved levada. Turning right (E) we follow the levada and in a few metres we are on the broad dirt path alongside the levada running in a broad concrete culvert; both sides of the levada are covered in a profusion of wild flowers. Almost immediately (4M) we come to a waterfall by the levada where we need to clamber down the steps, cross the watercourse, and climb back up to the levada path. From the path we have views down the Ribeira do João Gomes valley to Funchal and the sea, while close by the abundance of wild plants creates a colourful countryside setting. From these 'alpine' meadows we move into woodland, mimosa/acacia trees closing off the view as the levada turns left into a steep pocket in the valley wall. As we move towards the head of the pocket the old forest closes in around us, moss covering the inland cliff in this green environment. At the apex of the pocket the levada is paved over to carry storm-water from the steep ravine above us. We climb up steps to cross the black rock 'table', then down more steps to rejoin the levada path as it starts to run out of the steep valley. Again we come into an area where the old forest forms a green tunnel as we approach another pocket,

Walk 7 Tornos to Jasmin Tea House.

where the levada has again been bridged to protect it from storm-water. As we come out of this pocket the old forest gives way to tall eucalyptus trees giving an airy feel to our route. Just after passing an old door, with a path cut into the slope above us, we get views down the valley and onto the Romeiros road. A couple of minutes further on we get views across to the villages of Romeiros and Babosas just before passing caves in the cliff alongside the levada. Just past a section where the levada has been straightened we come to the 'levada bus stop' steps (35M). This is where we would start in bad weather, but it does mean missing the old forest section.

Continuing along the levada path we catch glimpses of Funchal through the trees and pass a barred roadway above us, with a dirt path dropping away to our right, before coming out of the trees into open countryside. Giant fennels are prominent on this section as we curve round the hillside to pass below an old house before the levada comes back amongst trees again. We curve around a pocket just before the levada bridges a rainwater gully as we approach the first houses of Choupana. Below us are ducks and a duck pond along with vegetable plots as we pass the first house, whose terrace forms the levada wall like a canal side dwelling. Past the house the levada disappears into a tunnel as our path takes us up to a tarmac lane with the sign "Levada dos Tornos"; Walk 8 comes down the lane and crosses our route at this point.

The original route through the Quinta do Pomar has now been closed off to the public so we walk up the lane to take a path at the edge of the estate. This path takes us around Quinta do Pomar and then meets the levada and we continue alongside the running water. Our routes takes us along above houses and cultivated plots with paths leading up to the levada and after passing below a large villa we cross a concrete lane. Back alongside the levada we are walking through a meadow landscape with our path lined with agapanthas until after turning at the head of a valley, the levada bridged as usual, our route comes back amongst trees. In contrast to the trees we pass behind an ugly building where a trail crosses the levada. We pass small abandoned buildings alongside the levada and several trails leading off our path as the noise of traffic heralds our arrival at the E-201 road (90M). Across the E-201 the levada continues on amongst the trees, though you could follow the road downhill for 600 metres to the street entrance of the Jasmin Tea

Walk 7 Tornos to Jasmin Tea House.

House. We follow the levada path to pass our finish point, signs down to the Jasmin Tea House, but decide to enjoy the stroll along the waterway with open views down to the main road as it snakes through Lombo da Quinta village in the valley below us. Passing a pink house we come to a bridge at the head of a small valley and then we are into another valley lined with pines and overlooking the E-102. Out of the pines we pass below the topmost houses of Lombo da Quinta, their access ways crossing our route, and continue on past houses set just below the levada before turning into another pocket dotted with village houses. This is the last pocket and eucalyptus and mimosa trees announce our arrival at the E-102 on a dangerous blind bend. Here we turn around to retrace our steps back to the stairs down to the Jasmin Tea House where we select one of the speciality teas from their huge range and tuck into home made scones and jam as a reward for our efforts.

8. DA SERRA WEST.

The Levada da Serra is one of Madeira's 'walking motorways' much used by day-trip operators. On this western section of the levada you are unlikely to meet these groups and can enjoy a relaxing country stroll through woodland with an abundance of wild flowers. Where the levada finishes we descend on steep cobbled lanes, through Choupana where you can join the route of Walk 7, down to Bar/Rest Miranda at the N°30 bus terminus. Plenty of shade along this route means that this route can be followed comfortably even on the hottest of days.

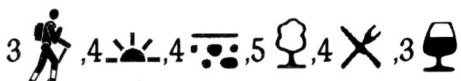

Time 2 hours, approx 6 kilometres.
Ascents 50 metres, descents 280 metres.

For once we are outside the region served by Funchal's city bus service and need to catch the country bus service N°29 or N°77 to Vale do Paraiso. Arriving at Vale do Paraiso we start by walking up the E-203 road signed to Poiso to pass the "O Paraiso" bar on our right (5M); the only refreshment opportunity on this route before reaching our finish. From the bar we continue up the road, passing a fenced stand of pines on our right, until we come to the pink walls and green

Walk 8 Da Serra West.

shutters of Casa do Reviver. Twenty metres further on we find the Levada da Serra where it crosses the E-203 main road. Walk 9 goes right (E) here in the direction of Camacha, while we turn left (W) to head towards Funchal.

We stroll along a wide dirt path following the 'dry' levada through woodland; in this area most of the water which was carried by the Levada da Serra is now diverted to the Levada dos Tornos lower down. The invigorating fragrances of eucalyptus and pine engulf us as we walk along the well shaded path and in less than a kilometre we come to views down onto Vale do Paraiso and our start on the E-203. The villages topmost houses are just below us, served by a concrete stair, as we pass a garage and stacks of willow wands. Keeping to the levada path we pass a small abandoned cottage just before crossing a cobbled road which leads up to Quinta Vale do Paraiso. In the quinta's ground are huge examples of ancient trees, quite a contrast to the younger tree growth we normally see on our walks. Leaving the quinta behind we come to a small tunnel where we climb over the tunnel to cross a stone path and fast running culvert before rejoining the levada. We curve right to views over water storage lakes down to the coast and then as we turn around the hillside we come back into woodland, mostly mimosa/acacia with agapanthus lining the path. We are now in older forest, emphasised by an old stone rampart above the levada at the apex of a pocket, and in the next pocket an old stone bridge spans the cleft at its head.

Leaving the bridge behind we come out of the old forest to walk between groves of tall eucalyptus, which give way to pines as round the valley. For once we are heading uphill, as the levada goes into a tunnel, onto an old stone road and then back down to rejoin the levada. Wild flowers are abundant on this section. Above us the whole hillside is covered in massive drifts of orange wild gladioli, while below us the gently wooded hillside runs down to houses in the valley. We emerge into the open to turn into another pocket with orange gladioli above our route and cultivated plots down below us. Leaving this pocket we round a hillside into another pocket, this time the path is lined with drifts of white gladioli while below us yellow broom add splashes of colour to the view. We pass through a stand of eucalyptus just before rounding a spur into another pocket where mimosas now line the path. The levada is very overgrown on this section and tall eucalyptus occupy the slopes above and below our route while the levada is covered with blue

Walk 8 Da Serra West.

flowered periwinkle.

Gradually the nature of our walk has changed from levada to woodland route, with the path prominent alongside the overgrown channel. Walking through tall eucalyptus the levada disappears before we come to a crossroads with a red path crossing our route and becoming a red dirt road going down on our left. We keep straight ahead on the path as it runs along a contour and the levada channel re-emerges alongside our route. Ferns, pea-flower and brambles line the route through this tranquil woodland as we continue in and out of small pockets in the hillside with forested slopes on both sides of us. We come to the western end of the unused levada to walk through woodland until our path swings right and runs onto a steep cobbled lane. From the end of the Levada da Serra our route is all downhill, easy walking but it can be tough on the knees and calves. We head down the cobbled lane beneath the tree canopy, mimosa and broom adding splashes of colour to the pine forest each side of us. We drop down the lane to meet the E-201 main road, crossing straight over to continue steeply down another steep lane, passing the "Campo do Pomar" football ground on our left. Our route twists down to the route of Walk 7 in Choupana, which offers alternative finishes at the Jasmin Tea House or Romeiros.

We continue on the shortest route to refreshments, steeply down hill on the lane through Choupana. Below the Quinta do Pomar the tarmac lane swings left while we continue on the old cobbled route which drops down between houses on our right and a wall on our left. As we go down the 'street' becomes even steeper until we drop down onto the newer tarmac road. Ahead the old cobbled route heads straight down past the Bar/Rest Miranda, while on our right is the main road up to Romeiros and the N°30 bus terminus; the N°29 bus also passes here. What more could you ask for at the end of a walk; Miranda's friendly bar, an interesting menu, superb views, a bus service for when you choose to return into town, and an interesting continuation - Walk 10 A Little Bit Of Everything.

9. DA SERRA EAST.

Another relaxing woodland stroll along the Levada da Serra, again starting from Vale do Paraiso but this time we head east towards the wickerwork centre of Camacha. On this section of the levada we pass through village outskirts, including a refreshment stop, as well as woodland. Much of the route is shaded making this a comfortable walk on hotter days. Unfortunately this is one of Madeira's most popular 'coach trip' walks, so if you don't want to find yourself behind fifty bumbling strollers start out early!

3 🚶 ,4 🌅 ,4 🍱 ,5 🌳 ,3 ✕ ,3 🍷

Time 2 hours, approx 7 kilometres.
Ascents 50 metres, descents 80 metres.

We have the same start point as Walk 8 using the 29 or 77 country bus to Vale do Paraiso, and then up the E-203 to the levada just above Casa do Reviver. If you are unfortunate to find a log-jam of tourist buses disgorging their punters take heart in that they are paying 4-6,000 escudos to follow the same route as you. We turn right off the road onto the levada path as it runs behind pink buildings, the first tree is signed 'Raid Hipico' showing this to be a horse riding trail. Paths run down to the pink 'holiday homes' and after a concrete path with street lights we swing left above a weed covered water cistern resembling a giant bath of pea soup to come into deciduous woodland. The path takes us round a small pocket giving views back to our starting point as we pass above an interesting pent roof cottage.

Great drifts of orange gladioli cover the slopes above our route, while below the path the trees are covered in lichen fed by moist winds coming up the valley. A couple of cottages stand above the levada as we come out of the woods to views down the valley over abandoned apple orchards. We pass a stone path heading upwards as we approach the head of a pocket, where we cross over a watercourse lined with coral plants. Paths lead off up the valley towards another bridge up above us as we head out of the pocket.

Our route snakes along the 700 metre contour line through a mixture of woodland and abandoned orchards. We cross another water runoff just before the levada disappears, reappearing as we come alongside a white breeze-block wall. Down below us now are cultivated plots and orchards with access paths down from the levada as we come to cross a

Walk 9 Da Serra West.

road just below the "Vivenda do Dom Vivier". Leaving the houses behind we enter deciduous woodland again before the slopes above us become covered in broom, bracken and agapanthus and the trees below our path give way to cultivated plots as we cross the access path to a house set above the levada. Coming out of this pocket we turn around a rock outcrop and trees close in on the path so that we find ourselves walking along under the shady canopy of oak trees. Coming out of the trees we emerge to open hillsides giving clear views down the valley before the trees again surround the path, though the growl of traffic from the E-102 running along below us is still present.

We come into a small pocket whose gentle bracken and gorse covered slopes give the appearance of a highland glen, and at its head a small bridge protects the levada from water erosion. Our path swings left above an abandoned building and the path is edged by agapanthus with occasional oak trees providing shade as we come to cross a cobbled road (50M VdParaiso, 30M on the levada) beside a level change in the levada. Across the road we come under ancient oaks while down below us houses are glimpsed through the stands of eucalyptus. We swing left into a valley where the slopes have been cleared of trees and houses stand above the levada with entry gates onto our route. As we leave this valley drifts of white gladioli and agapanthus surround the last of the houses and concrete stairs run across the levada and down into the valley below as we turn into another pocket. This is another small valley with cleared slopes and we soon turn out of it into a more pleasing landscape of yellow broom and oak trees lining the path as we come above the E-102 main road. Steps lead to houses above the levada and concrete stairs run down towards the village below us as our path curves away from the main road into mixed woodland with excellent specimens of wild flowers enhancing our route. Oak trees continue to line the path before the woodland gives way to grass covered slopes dotted with pines. Turning at the head of the valley, by a small spring, we are back in a mixture of tall eucalyptus, mimosas and occasional pines as we move out of this valley.

Our path swings left for us to face a village across the valley from us as a path crosses the levada on a wooden bridge. We follow the levada path into the valley with ancient trees lining our route and giant fennels alongside the path. As the levada turns at the head of the valley we have a superb vista of wild plants continuing up the valley before we head

Walk 9 Da Serra East.

directly for the village. Our path meanders between the village houses, widening out to a concrete lane as concrete steps take us down onto a tarmac lane. Turning left we walk gently uphill alongside the levada channel, the levada disappearing into a pipe as we continue along to the welcoming sight of Bar Moises (a clean, comfortable refreshment stop) at a crossroads. From Bar Moises we go left on a lane marked as 'no through road' to meet the levada again. The road narrows as we leave the village and big oak trees line the route as we swing left round a red house to return to a woodland setting. Through ranks of eucalyptus and slender pines we get glimpses of a village ahead of us, getting clear views as we swing out of the trees. Houses with colourful gardens stand above the levada as we come into the small valley. Approaching the head of the valley we pass an access stair and the levada disappears into a tunnel as it turns across the apex. Yellow broom surrounds an abandoned cottage as we head out of the valley to come into the village alongside a large black boulder wall. We pass two garages just before the path widens enough for vehicle access and we come onto a cobbled road crossing the levada.

The normal finish (for tour parties) is down the cobbled lane to the centre of Camacha. However if you are still fresh we recommend following the levada around the particularly beautiful valley to the village of Rochao. The levada disappears as we come to the village's first houses and our path climbs up to a parking area. Continuing up from the parking area we come onto the tarmac lane leading up to Pedras do Rochao and the new, and virtually unused, road which heads around the next valley. The levada finally re-emerges on a dirt road next to a willow wand factory. The walking is easy in this area so you can take your choice of how far to stroll. As the tour parties finish in Camacha this section of the levada is comparatively quiet.

If you follow the cobbled road down to Camacha keep to the road, don't be tempted by steps going down, to join the E-102 just behind the church. A couple of minutes down the road brings us to the touristy centre of Camacha, very lively for the sunday market, and bus stops for the 29 or 77 bus.

10. A LITTLE BIT OF EVERYTHING.

Having skittered down Caminho do Meio to the Miranda bar/rest at Foguete on Walk 8, you could catch the N°30 bus, down past Jardim Botanico and into town. An alternative is to continue dropping straight down Caminho do Meio, and we do mean DROP, as it is 1 in 4 all the way down to Jardim Botanico. Having arrived at Miranda's and refreshed ourselves, why not try our unusual route? It takes a bit longer but it has countryside, trees, little hamlets, staired descents, alleys and a little bit of uphill.

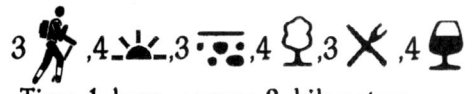

3 🚶 ,4 ☀ ,3 🏘 ,4 🌳 ,3 ✖ ,4 🍷

Time 1 hour, approx 3 kilometres.
Ascents 40 metres, descents 220 metres.

From Miranda's we set out in an unlikely direction by going right along Caminho das Voltas, until it turns left uphill. Alongside a 3.5 sign we take the concrete path past an overgrown hut, N°118, to descend into a small valley. Leaving behind the cultivated plots, we drop steeply down into the valley and turn around a large olive tree. On the far side of the valley we are amongst the woods and climb steadily to a grove of mature eucalyptus trees. At the peak we come amongst the soaring trunks, and our path is joined by a concrete stair coming down the hillside. Turning left, we round the hillside to meet a stairway which drops us into a new valley. We head towards two houses past mimosa trees and a profusion of wild flowers. At the houses our path turns right and runs downhill with views over Funchal and the coast. Down a concrete stair past house N°21, and a path goes off left. We continue the steep staired descent between houses until we reach a small wooden gate where the alley turns sharp right. Sharp left, and we are onto the second stairway which takes us down to a tarmaced road, with the sign, "Escadas da Travesa do Pomar" - Stairway to Pomar. We turn left on the road and look for house N°25 where we take a stairway heading steeply down. After houses, the stair runs down between plots until we meet post N°10 where the path turns sharp right. On the flat until the imposing gates of N°1 mark a left turn back onto a staired descent. At the path's next junction we leave the path to go right along a flat alley running between houses and a wall. We come to a sign ENT45 as we go down three steps, and our route starts sloping into a ravine with views down to Funchal.

Walk 10 A Little Bit of Everything.

We come around the pocket of the ravine in front of house N°62 to head gently uphill. At house N°40 we come to a steep tarmac road where we turn down the road to the stairway, "Pareda Bela Vista" just twenty metres from N°40. We head down the steep stair to a parking area in the valley below us. At the valley floor is a quaint traditional house away on the left, as we start the stiff hundred metre climb, coming above a traditional house with a fine Canarian palm in its garden. We stroll along the road enjoying views over Funchal, until we come to the Caminho do Meio running steeply downhill. At this point you could head straight down the caminho to Jardim Botanico, but we will indulge in a little more sightseeing. We go uphill (yes, uphill!) for 150 metres, and gratefully turn left onto Vereda do Cliffe Choupana opposite a small shop. A few steps bring us above a pair of villas, to pass plots and house N°35. We come to steep steps climbing to a road above us, but rather than climb these, we go down and left onto a hardly-used path which passes in front of a cave. The path changes from concrete to dirt as we duck under grape vines which cover this countrified section of our route. The path meanders along, until we join a stair-effect path to go downhill, reaching the skeleton of an old house where we turn right. We pass small houses and vegetable plots, until the path drops down a stone stair-effect section in front of a breeze block wall. On this section, take care as you may bump your head on someone's doorstep! In this narrow alley, we drop down giant steps under the doorstep; it's not every day you'll see a front entry like that! We emerge from the alley by the blue painted wall of N°2C, to turn right. A concrete path brings us onto the main road by houses 40, 42 and 44. For once we follow the main road downhill until we see the Vereda do Jardim Botanico on our left. We leave the road for a pleasant stroll along the path as it curves gently round the hillside. In a couple of minutes we come to a road and sign, "Vereda do Jardim Botanico" pointing back the way we have come. We are now back on Caminho do Meio with just a couple of hundred metres to skitter downhill to the Botanical Gardens - well, we never said it was the most direct route.

11. CAMACHA TO JASMIN TEA HOUSE.

This walk comes from Roy Chambers at The Jasmin Tea House, so it is not surprising that it finishes at this popular/unique refreshment stop. You can link the walk in with routes 7 and 6 to make a Camacha to Monte route.

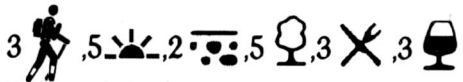

3 🚶 ,5 ⛅ ,2 🍽 ,5 🌳 ,3 ✕ ,3 🍷

Time 2 hours, approx 6 kilometres.
Ascents negligible, descents 120 metres.

We start by taking the 29 or 77 bus to Camacha and get off at the Galp Petrol Station just before reaching Camacha. Following the traffic sign for Caniço we go down the tarmac road (S) under the new Camacha road. Approximately 10 minutes down the road we come to a new housing development on our right which we turn off into(SW). Passing a bar on our left we follow the road past breathtaking views down across the terraced valley to the coastline at Caniço. Descend the first set of steps on the left (opposite a large white house) to come onto the levada and turn right (W). After a short distance note the collection of wicker for sale by João Batista Carreira and be sure to see his unique wicker violins which are found nowhere else on the Island.

After 30 minutes, look across the valley and see how the massive landslide smashed through the levada which then had to be piped across the break. At the cobbled road bear left and follow the levada through the lovely "Paradise Valley". Depending upon the time of year, you can see many different wild flowers as well as plants introduced to the Island such as agapanthus, hydrangea, fuchsia and valerian. At 45 minutes we come to the tunnel. If you have a good torch you can continue through the tunnel, fifteen minutes until you emerge into the world again. An alternative is to climb up the path which leads over the tunnel.

Once past the tunnel, continue to the road and turn left for a short distance before turning right at a factory building with large green doors and follow a concrete road until re-joining the levada on your left; at this point there is a good view across the Blandy reservoir. After 90-105 minutes we reach the main road at a sharp bend. Take great care crossing the road and rejoin the levada. Follow the levada for 25 minutes through stands of eucalyptus trees, orchards and wild flowers until reaching the steps which lead down to the Jasmin Tea House. Down the steps and you can refresh yourself from the

Walk 11 Camacha to Jasmin Tea House.

massive selection of teas, possibly supplemented with home-made scones and jam.

12. LEVADA DO CANIÇAL (West).

Levada walking is popular with many visitors to Madeira. In the east of the Island the Levada do Caniçal is the most popular "easy" route. If you want to avoid the crowds either start early or in the late afternoon. Early on the route is slightly vertiginous with unguarded drops alongside the path but once past these it is easy walking through glorious contryside accompanied by abundant endemic flora.

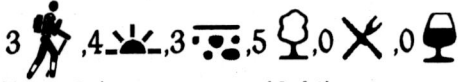

3 ,4 ,3 ,5 ,0 ,0

Time 3 hours, approx 12 kilometres.
Ascents 40 metres, descents negligible.

From Machico town square we take the 156 bus (130 escudos) up to its terminus near the top of Maroços. From the bus pull in we go over the river on a concrete bridge to face the route's only climb up a long concrete stair between the village houses. At the top of the stair (3M but seems longer) we come onto the levada, paved at this point, to head east. The top end of Maroços is randomly developed with a mixture of attractive houses and "self-builts" clinging to the steep side of the valley. Our route is along the levada following a contour line which bisects the steeply terraced valley wall and soon the concrete is replaced by a dirt path (muddy in wet weather). Turning across a sharp cleft we pass a spring which crosses the levada (6M). On the next section the levada path has an unguarded drop beside it, requiring careful footwork and which may disturb vertigo sufferers. Past this section we pass around a promontory lined with houses to turn into another pocket in the valley wall, concrete stairways crossing the levada to access the houses in this area (10M). Our progress continues in a leisurely manner (unless muddy) as the levada keeps to its contour to snake into and out of pockets in the valley wall. A wooden "Hansel & Gretel" bridge cuts off the final loop at the head of one pocket notable for its stands of eucalyptus trees (18M). The levada brings us back above the main village of Maroços to pass through a clutch of housing and come into a small

Walk 12 Levada do Caniçal (West).

pocket with a cascading waterfall at its head (28M).
Back in the main valley we come to a bluff protruding from the valley wall which is tiered with self-built housing to turn into a sharp cleft, with unguarded drops beside the levada requiring careful footwork on this section (41M). In contrast to the shanty built bluff, immaculate traditional cottages are ahead of us, which we pass (45M) to walk into the head of this sharp valley. At the head of the valley bowls of fruit are placed for sale (oranges 50esc) and a sign board announces "O Tunel do Caniçal 9km", "Maroços 3km" (50M). Pines hide the main valley from view until we emerge from the trees to turn into another pocket, this one dotted with houses. Careful footwork is required where the levada runs alongside a cliff-face with a severe drop below the path (63M), and following a man-made cave we pass through a short tunnel. For some time we have been away from human habitation but now we come back to houses set below the levada (77M) and abandoned terraces. Following a substantial water runoff bridged over the levada we walk through trees to pass through an area of terraces, some in cultivation, to the head of the pocket where steps cut off a small loop of the levada (95M). As we come out of this pocket we come to a water tap and the unexpected sight of a new warehouse alongside the levada (98M), which is served by a newly cut dirt lane. After the rural charms of the Ribeira das Cales and Ribeira Grande valleys the levada brings us round to overlook the extensively housed valley of Ribeira Seca (107M).

We pass through a small pocket with kennels of howling hunting dogs (110M) and a water tap (dated 20/8/98) to head up into the Ribeira da Noia valley. Gradually the housing density reduces as we leave Ribeira Seca behind and the slopes become tree-lined in places. Another public water tap is found at the head of a side valley (123M) and soon the valley floor drops sharply away on our right as the levada cuts across a craggy cliff-face. As the cliff recedes views open up down into the Machico valley and we pass self-built houses set below the levada (135M). We turn into a pocket, at the head of which a substantial stone stair leads up to a large, traditional barn (140M). Back in the main valley we find ourselves walking below rugged cliffs with a severe drop at the edge of the levada path for a short section. The levada winds along the side of the Ribeira Seca valley until mimosa/acacia woods mark the change to a beaten red earth path which curves around towards the tunnel. Our final stage is marked by the sight of a bright lime house as we walk

29

Walk 12 Levada do Caniçal (West).

along to Vivienda Oliveira just before we come down to the main road by the tunnel entrance and bus stop (180M).

13. A PEAK EFFORT.

If your image of Madeiran walking is of easy strolling along levadas, then this route along the old path between Machico and Caniçal is definitely outside your imagination. A steep climbing ascent is rewarded with terrific views and followed by a superb wild landscape for our descent to Caniçal; making this a route for the more energetic. You can link this route with Walk 14 for an "eastern tour" and with Walk 12 (using the lane to Pico do Facho) for a Machico or Caniçal finish.

4 🚶 ,5 ☀ ,3 🌧 ,4 🌳 ,1 ✕ ,2 🍷

Time 2 hours, approx 7 kilometres.
Ascents 310 metres, descents 310 metres.

Starting from Machico town square we head over the bridge into the square of Banda de Além, where we turn left (N) to walk up a narrow cobbled street of small shops parallel to the river. We pass a chemist (farmacia) on our left and the police station on our right to come up to a junction where the cobbles are replaced by tarmac (5M). The street continues on but we turn right (NE) in front of Auto Milagres Tyre garage to go steeply uphill on a tarmac lane. Ahead we can see the transmitter towers on Pico do Facho and the two electricity pylons which roughly mark our route over the pass. A steep climb brings us up onto a higher street opposite tiny cotages set amongst new developments (9M). We turn downhill for 50 metres to another junction marked by a public water tap to swing left for another steep climb up a lane past a school. The climb continues upwards towards an imposing new development as we cross a concrete walkway (the route of Walk 15) running along the top level of Machico's houses. Just before we reach the edge of the new development we leave the concrete lane to step right onto a narrow barely-worn path which climbs up the right hand side of the development. In places parts of the original boulder-laid trail show through the grass as we climb up the steep slopes, the electricity pylons giving the general direction of our route ahead. From the back of the development the path, almost

Walk 13 A Peak Effort.

stepped in places, curves left before swinging right to head directly for the first pylon (28M). The path curves left again (N), crossing the slope diagonally and now more clearly defined by the remains of a boulder wall, to swing right (E) below a rock outcrop for us to head between the two pylons (34M). On our eastern traverse we come above the first pylon to reach a collapsed boulder wall where the trail swings (ENE) up past a corrugated iron hut towards the second pylon (42M). As we approach the pass, and second pylon, the original path is replaced by a twisting climb up onto the new tarmac lane serving Pico do Facho (47M).

After that steep, relentless ascent (300 metres) we take a small diversion to follow the lane for a steady climb up to the picnic area set below the peak. From this little used mirador we have splendid views across to Porto Santo and the Desertas islands, along with the tourist jets passing below on their landing approach to Funchal airport. Unfortunately the peak is occupied by the fenced transmitter station, but this still doesn't stop us enjoying the best views along this section of eastern Madeira and all too soon it is time to get back onto the route.

Strolling back down the lane we come to our upward route (0M) to begin our descent into Caniçal. We follow a path (NE), marked by a red waymark on a boulder in the cliff, gently down past heaps of spoil. Once past the spoil heaps excellent views open up over the peninsula as we curve around the hillside; noticeably more rugged than the landscape of our ascent. Below us are cultivated terraces as we keep to the narrow path heading generally towards the wind farm (NE). We pass smudgy brown banded rock on our left as we keep to the main path, ignoring a smaller path off to our right, to come above a pylon. Our path curves north to swing around and above a steep valley which drops down to the sea. We begin to descend, quite steeply at first before levelling out in the bowl of the valley below some traditional huts. The path begins to lose its rocky nature and is now edged by the remains of a stone wall. Our route clings to the bowl of the valley above the steep cleft down to the sea, its boulder-laid nature reasserting itself again. We come below a multi-coloured hut (8M) as we continue to curve round the valley, climbing gently towards tree-dotted slopes and a bare ridge marked by an electricity pylon. The path becomes narrower and steeper, pushing through white heather as we come up onto the windy, bare ridge alongside the pylon (17M). The path has a small discontinuity on the ridge so we

Walk 13 A Peak Effort.

go left for a few metres to find its continuation for us to drop down into the next valley, where agriculture must have been abandoned decades ago. We go down through a fire damaged acacia/mimosa wood where the narrow dirt path requires careful footwork. Emerging from the trees we descend steadily between long abandoned terraces around the bowl of the valley. Our path becomes rougher, and brambles push in on our route (secateurs useful), as we head ENE between stone walls to round a rocky ridge into a smaller, but steeper valley (24M). Impressive rock walls run around this long abandoned valley, sometimes used by a local farmer to graze his small herd of cows, as our path narrows and descends as it heads seawards (E) down the side of the valley. Just as it seems that the path will continue towards the sea it turns (NE) in the direction of Caniçal (32M). The path divides at a sheet of rock; we stay on the upper path, marked with red and orange waymarks, for a gentle ascent along the top of a boulder wall - take care where small bushes try to push you off the wall (secateurs useful). As we come alongside a rock outcrop the peninsula comes into view, and on rounding the outcrop we look down on Caniçal (36M). Our path now runs inland (N) under the outcrop, climbing gently before descending quite steeply in zig-zags towards the beach to the west of Caniçal. We come over a stone ridge (43M) to continue down, the path turning inland for a gentle stroll across grassy slopes to go around a valley cleft slashed into the Island's mountainous side. Our route continues down past the remains of old walls in the direction of the centre of Caniçal. We come above the inlet at the western end of the pebble beach. Our path becomes rockier and requires concentration as we drop down towards the head of the inlet, a steep scrambling descent finally bringing us down to a stone bridge over the inlet's watercourse (56M). Over the bridge a muddy section of path brings us onto the rough dirt lane which runs down to the beach. Climbing up the lane we come a fenced farming area below a sports stadium. Turning right we follow a rough path down the side of the fencing to come down onto a tarmac road, its inland section lined by palms. Five minutes along the road we come to the old fishing section of Caniçal where we curve uphill to finish outside the small church and bus stop (70M).

14. LEVADA DO CANIÇAL (East).

Few people realise that the Levada do Caniçal continues beyond the tunnel and even fewer walk this route. While the start (beneath a quarry) and finish (down a featureless dirt road into Caniçal's poorer housing) are unimpressive the main part of the route is through beautiful countryside and woodland. You can also add this route to Walk 12 and Walk 13, by walking through the tunnel and using the new Pico do Facho lane, to increase your walking options in the eastern region. A short section near the start has unprotected drops alongside the levada path which might disturb vertigo sufferers.

3 🚶 ,5 🍽 ,3 🚌 ,5 🍹 ,1 ✗ ,2 🍷

Time 1.5 hours, approx 5.5 kilometres.
Ascents 20 metres, descents 230 metres.

We reach our start at the eastern end of the Caniçal tunnel on the 113 bus from Machico town square; press the bell before the bus emerges from the tunnel. Beside the eastern tunnel entrance stone stairs lead up to a small shrine, while lower down the Levada do Caniçal leaves the road. We follow the narrow path alongside the small levada to cross the access road to the quarry set just above our route. Metal handrails provide protection from a sharp drop just before we cross a second access road (4M); you can cut this section by walking up the access road from the main road. A stream is crossed (7M) as we start to move along below the quarry's rock wall and passing a culvert taking water down from the levada. Our path narrows, and requires careful footwork, as we work our way along a section with an unprotected drop on the right of the path; concentrating on your footsteps means you should notice the "1955" date written into the levada wall. Passing a "Beware of falling rocks" sign (12M) the path becomes less vertiginous as it runs along the top of a boulder wall before we meet another section of unprotected drop where the levada and path cling to a cliff face (17M). There are excellent views on this section, with the road far below us, but do 'Stop to Look at the View'! The path improves as we round a bluff to head north across grassy slopes before turning into the Cova Grande valley by a water change point (20M).

Now the levada channel is filled with black pipe, rather than running water, as we follow a contour to meet the valley's watercourse. At this point the levada is protected by a broad

Walk 14 Levada do Caniçal (East).

swathe of concrete, below which we can see the sculpting effects of water erosion down the valley (25M). Soon the black pipe ends for us to walk beside running water again to pass two juniper trees as our route curves north above the uppermost houses of Caniçal. The hillside becomes steeper, and wilder, as the levada curves left (NW) into another valley. Ahead are cultivated terraces and traditional huts as a broad dirt lane climbs up to meet our route. Crossing the dirt lane we follow the levada above the topmost hut to swing left into mature woodland. Pines, mimosa/acacia and yellow broom make this one of Madeira's prettiest, but possibly least known, sections of woodland. We follow the southern side of the tree filled valley to come to a levada bridge over the valley's watercourse (38M). You have three choices; walk across on the narrow walls of the levada (not recommended), scramble down to the stream bed and up the other side (uncomfortable), or step into the levada to wade across the bridge (our choice in walking sandals footwear).

After taking a break to clean our feet we set off again (E) under the woodland canopy to come into the open again (44M) to fine views over the peninsula. Our route is now through open woodland curving into a new valley where eucalyptus trees feature along with junipers. The levada crosses the valley floor to head out (ENE) past the remains of stone built huts and terraces (50M) and a water runoff bridged over the levada. Emerging from the woodland (S) we have views over tree filled valleys to Caniçal's "Free Port" industrial zone. In another couple of minutes (56M) we are negotiating a fallen tree. We are in another tree filled valley, the levada almost overgrown by plants. Crossing the head of the valley by a water runoff and a ring-barked eucalyptus the plants now almost cover the waterway and we have to take care not to step into the channel as we pass between earth banks (60M). We come (E) into an area of cleared woodland where a small culvert takes water from the levada, the culvert running straight down the hillside on our right, just before the levada swings right (SE) to run downhill alongside a dirt roadway. Our final stage is down the dirt road, passing water eroded slopes on our right and a domed water reservoir on our left (70M), following the industrial zone fence. We come to our first houses as the road becomes tarmac surfaced and runs down to a junction by the post office (correios) and free port entrance gates (80M). Going straight over the junction we walk down the street and follow it right to come down to

Walk 14 Levada do Caniçal (East).

Caniçal's church and some well earned refreshments (85M).

15. ALL-WEATHER STROLLING.

Levada walking can be a very muddy experience in wet weather, but all is not lost if you encounter Madeiran rainfall. Here we have a 'town' route all on hard all-weather surfaces, concrete or tarmac, suitable for trainers and with plenty of refreshment opportunities along the way - just the route for you while waiting for the countryside to dry out!

Time 2 hours, approx 8 kilometres.
Ascents 150 metres, descents 150 metres.

Starting from Machico's square we walk over the bridge into the square of Banda de Além (literally - the other side of the river), where we turn left to head inland along the cobbled street. At the health food shop we turn right to head up a steep street which has the sign "Aluvião 3/11/1956" on its corner (3M). It is a steep climb up to a junction by a public water point for us to turn left and continue uphill (NNW). After 40 metres we turn right to climb another steep street (NE), which gets noticeably steeper as we come up to a blue painted, graffiti covered, wall at its top (12M). Our "Hillside Picnic" option goes right at this point. We head left (WNW) on a small tarmac lane that runs between houses and soon becomes a concrete path running along a contour at the upper limit of Machico's housing development. We cross the route of Walk 13 (15M) just below the newest, and highest, development in the town as we head north on the concrete walkway. Traditional huts are set below the path just before we turn into a cleft where a small concrete bridge takes us over the watercourse (17M). The path crosses the top of a steep cobbled lane just before we come to a large modern house. the surprising feature of this house is its double gates and garage; but how do you get a car to the house? Our elevated stroll continues through the higher houses with views down over the populated valley below us on our left until the path ends at a long concrete stairway overlooking a sharp cleft (25M). Here we go left down the stairs to come

Walk 15 All-Weather Strolling.

onto a tarmac lane which is bridged over the cleft and its watercourse. Turning right (N) we continue our stroll as the lane climbs gently up past a shop and bar to pass a crumbling (self-built?) villa adorned with various statuary. Our lane meanders uphill past impressive new villas and the snack bar Migaro. As the gradient increases we pass a concrete lane on our left before climbing up to meet the main road (40M).

We carefully cross over the main road to walk up a tarmac lane past "Entrada de Larano" shop and bar and a gentle uphill stroll takes us into the Ribeira Seca valley past a mixture of housing and terraced plots. From a distance, such as on the Levada do Caniçal, Ribeira Seca seems to be made up mostly of identikit modern houses. At close quarters we see that all the houses are different and many incorporate a certain degree of quirkiness. This is illustrated by a house below a bus stop (52M) where the rooftop parking area is accessed by a 45° degree semi-staired driveway. We pass up through a bus turning circle and then the lane runs gently downhill for a while. There are plenty of refreshment stops along this route as the lane undulates along the valley wall for us to come to the Bar Boca do Risco (60M); opposite which is the stairway route of Walk 16. Another couple of minutes sees the lane cross the head of the valley and start to run down the western wall. Steep, stepped access ways drop down to cross the watercourse and then climb up the opposite wall to provide links between the two sides of the valley. At 69M we come across another example of quirkiness and extreme parking. On the left of the lane is a small garage supported on stilts and next to this is a small house with a Toyota minibus parked on its roof. There is no connection between the roof and the lane, the minibus having been driven across the drop on steel rails - a rather troublesome manoeuvre when you want to go out for a drive!

With the lane and access stairways you can gently stroll as far as you like through this interesting urban/rural landscape. We choose to return to the eastern side by turning down a steep tarmac lane, with a shop on its corner, for a skittery descent down between houses, a school and a church to come to a turning area alongside the watercourse. Across a pedestrian bridge we climb up stairs to come onto a broad concrete walkway which we follow (SE) along the side of the valley. The walkway curves towards Machico for us to come up onto a tarmac lane behind a church. Walking around the church we come to its main facade and square, both being

Walk 15 All-Weather Strolling.

refurbished in March 99 (87M). After admiring the church's new handiwork we head up the steep lane to carefully cross over the main road and take coffee in the "O Crespo" bar (92M). After refreshment we take a steep concrete lane running up the side of the bar and in a couple of minutes find ourselves on the tarmac lane of our outward route. From this point we retrace our outward route for an easy stroll back to Machico, with the option to follow the quiet lane all the way into Banda de Além or take the pedestrian walkway of our outward route (120M).

16. BOCA DO RISCO.

Boca da Risco, 'the dangerous gate', is a popular walking destination. Unlike other guides we start at the Ribeira Seca bus stop, saving thirty minutes each way on the journey. Using this route means that you can combine it with Walks 12 & 15 to add to the variety of walks in this region. Walking up to Boca do Risco is straightforward but the path is narrow and slightly vertiginous in places. in wet weather the path becomes muddy and slippery(!), so we only recommend that you walk when the ground is dry.

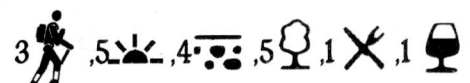

Time 2 hours, approx 7 kilometres.
Ascents 200 metres, descents 200 metres.

We start by taking the Caniçal (113) bus (or Walk 15). As the bus climbs up the valley wall past the "O Crespo" bar (on the right) to swing right round a hairpin bend press the bell and the bus stops where Walk 15 crosses the main road. Follow the route of Walk 15 into Ribeira Seca until you reach Bar Boca do Risco (15M). Opposite the bar we climb up steep concrete steps (NE) to a crossroads of paths where we continue straight ahead up more steep concrete steps (little used). This steep ascent twists round the wall of a newish cottage, behind which the steps end for us to continue on a dirt and rock path (20M). Now we have a relaxed ascent following the path past narrow cultivated plots before tackling a steep zig-zag through rock and then reach a Y-junction. We take the main path right to keep climbing upwards to where a flight of concrete steps takes us up onto

Walk 16 Boca do Risco.

the Levada do Caniçal (23M). Remember this point; the levada swings sharp left south of the steps, if you want to return by our 'unconventional' route.

After that steep ascent we now have an easy stroll (N) along the levada until we reach the conventional trail, which can be seen trudging up the valley below us, just past and above a tiled cottage with a collapsed tiled roof hut above it (30M). Stone steps across the levada mark our route to steadily ascend the dirt and rock path (NE). Ignoring side paths into the terraces we keep climbing steadily to come through a grove of mimosa/acacia trees (35M) to the sight of cultivated terraces filling a pocket in the valley's eastern wall. Now our route becomes a narrow brown ribbon of a path which contours (slightly vertiginously) above the vigorously growing vegetables. Turning out of the pocket we carefully cross an eroded section to pass above a hut and cultivated terraces (37M). We walk through slopes carpeted with yellow flowering clover and dotted with mimosa and white heather. Our route turns (E) into a large pocket of wild countryside in the valley wall. We walk into the sharp cleft to cross the watercourse (40M) with the path becoming rockier until it curves back to wind through tall pines lining the main valley. The path swings right into another pocket filled with pines, and with beautiful wild hillsides at the head of the pocket. Across the watercourse (46M) we climb up the northern side to come above the trees by a marker stone; with RNV and an arrow on its side away from the path.

Now we are back in the main valley as we walk up towards huts and cultivated terraces. Just before reaching the huts, the first a noisy dog pen, we go left (W) at a junction in the trail following a "Boca do Risco" sign set on a large rock (51M). Soon we are back heading north on a long steady climb which brings us up to the natural gate in the rock ridge that is the Boca do Risco (57M). Through the gate we have spectacular views (in good weather) along Madeira's northern coastline. Beyond the Boca do Risco is the 'northern coastal path' (marked by an orange square and two stars) which descends (E) to the steep agricultural settlement of Larano; this route should only be undertaken in good weather by experienced walkers with no fear of vertigo. If you do get caught by the rain at Boca do Risco there is a large man-made cave just to the west of the pass to shelter in. Our return is back down our outward route to Ribeira Seca, with careful foot work on the narrow sections.

17. DESCENT FROM PORTELA.

Portela is one of the finest mirador viewpoints which is easily accessible by bus (53) from Machico. Until quite recently (1996) the route from Portela down to Maroços was a walking route, but the lower section is now a new road - presumably to serve the new road tunnel when it is completed. This is still an enjoyable route, particularly if combined with Walk 18 or with sections of Walks 12, 15 and 16 for a long distance route finishing in Machico.

2 🚶 ,4 ☀ ,2 🚌 ,4 🛏 ,0 🍴 ,0 🍷

Time 1 hour, approx 4 kilometres.
Ascents negligible, descents 400 metres.

Arriving at the Portela pass we take a few minutes admiring the view down over Eagle Rock and Porto da Cruz, and perhaps taking coffee in the Miradouro da Portela, before setting off. Our start is on the north side of the mirador heading east on the dirt road to a junction (2M) where we go right to come onto a forest road with the sign "Fonte de Vemelhe" and "Maroços - Machico". Following the sign we walk down the dirt road, passing a track off to our right, with a small water channel running along on our left. Tall eucalyptus trees rise up from a bluff on our left as the water channel disappears underground and our route winds along below a tree clad ridge to the north of us. On our right we have occasional views through the trees across the sharp valley to the main road. Stately eucalyptus trees are a feature of this section, their heady fragrance adding to our enjoyment of the route. The forest road runs along a contour (approx S) with some gentle downhill sections until it swings left (ENE) to give us views down to the sea (13M). Now the descent becomes steeper as we pass a rough dirt lane which climbs up to the "Fonte de Vemelhe" (15M), and we are going seriously downhill through the forest, twisting along beneath earth cliffs until we drop down (S) to come to a street light and the first house (22M).

Cottages and cultivated terraces line the eastern side of the dirt lane until the lane swings left (E, 26M) to continue its descent amongst cultivated terraces. We go through a hairpin bend (30M) to overlook a tarmac road and steep cultivated terraces climbing up the opposite side of a sharp cleft to the eucalyptus tree line. A skittering steep descent, through another hairpin bend drops us down to meet the tarmac (32M). From this point you have a choice of setting out on

Walk 17 Descent From Portela.

our "Quiet Forest" circular route, or of turning right (W) and heading towards the centre of Ribeira de Machico. It is an easy stroll along the almost traffic free lane through this dispersed agricultural community to come to the road junction by the church and school (40M). From here we can turn right to head uphill to the main road and its bus stop (47M). Our normal finish is to walk down the new steep (and very steep) road to pass above the new road tunnel (in construction) and two industrial sites to come to the Levada do Caniçal on the left of the road at the top end of Maroços (55M). This steep road, constructed in 1996, has obliterated the original walking route which used to link these two communities; such is the price of progress.

18. THE QUIET FOREST.

Above the settlement of Maroços wooded hills and ridges rise up to meet the island's rugged north coast. Several "unmapped" trails access this large area of endemic woodland, mostly logging trails but also up to the fire watch tower on Larano peak. Here you can enjoy Madeira's forest on good trails without finding hordes of "coach-borne" day trippers spoiling the tranquility; long may this forgotten corner remain that way. Tree species vary depending upon the wetness of each valley; eucalyptus and mimosa/acacia in the drier valleys, laurel and juniper in the wetter valleys. You can walk for hours on these forest trails, as we know very well, but if you do decide to leave our route do remember your way back!

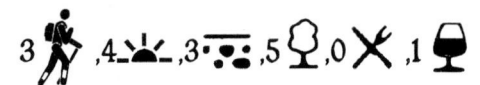

Time 3 hours, approx 11 kilometres.
Ascents 190 metres, descents 180 metres.

From where Walk 17 reaches the tarmac lane we turn left (E) to climb up past an 'angular' self-built set on a promontory overlooking the steep valley. It is a steady climb up past 'treasure chest' crash barriers to reach a crest of the lane. Our route swings around another sharp cleft and resumes climbing up to another crest in the lane (8M). Now we stroll gently downhill through meadows dotted with cottages to pass the only bar on this route (11M); car drivers should park

Walk 18 The Quiet Forest.

along this section. Shortly after the bar the tarmac finishes for us to continue on a wide dirt road (13M) which swings left and contours round a pocket in the valley wall. We pass a dirt lane dropping away to our right as we stroll along beneath abandoned terraces and old huts. As the dirt road turns from one pocket to another we come to a small viewpoint to look straight down the valley to Machico (18M). So far the dirt road has been contouring around the valley wall but now it starts to run gently downhill past stately eucalyptus trees and hillsides packed with masses of endemic flora. We continue downhill beneath a section of old terraces (22M) and then as the road swings left we pass an old logging trail blocked off with pine trunks (24M), followed by another dirt road dropping into the valley on our right (28M). So far the dirt road has been well endowed with local flora but now our route becomes truly forested as we swing around the head of a tree-filled valley and start climbing up the northern wall. We pass an eye-catching example of orange lichen/moss on the earth wall before turning into another valley in the forest. Now the dirt road runs gently downhill and the eucalyptus have given way to tall pines and laurels. Across the head of the valley we climb gently up to a junction where a wide dirt road comes up through the trees to join us (38M); this is our return route after a circuit of the forest.

Keeping to the main roadway we head west into another steep, tree filled valley with red and white transmitter towers atop the ridge above our route. Across the head of the valley a steady climb (NE) takes us up past a graffiti carved earth cliff (48M) and our route keeps climbing gently, or steadily, as it twists in and out of pockets in the valley wall. Botanists should keep a careful watch for the sharp cleft containing classic specimens of giant fern (58M and more usually seen as unusual garden plants) on this section of our route. Up through a cutting and eventually the roadway runs downhill through a more open section of forest with views over the Machico valley. We swing down into another valley and cross its head (63M) to climb steadily up to a mirador viewpoint (65M). West of us the transmitter towers mark the end of an unusual ridge topped with tall trees which seem which glow eerily against the skyline when seen from this angle. Bracken and brambles have taken over the cleared areas alongside our route as we climb up to a major junction of dirt roads and a metal post which once held signboards (68M).

Walk 18 The Quiet Forest.

The main roadway continues uphill as we take the right dirt road to start descending before climbing up to a pass marked by a line of juniper trees. On the pass a grassy trail runs south along the line of junipers to a turning circle. We keep on the dirt road to walk down into a forest valley noticeable for its rocky cliffs, as compared to earth banks elsewhere (83M). Across the head of the valley we climb gently at first, then steadily, and finally steeply (SSW) up to a junction (95M). We take the minor dirt road to the right to drop down into the forest. A steady descent (W) twists us down past a steep dirt lane up to our left to a T-junction (105M).

We go right (W) to drop down past tall pines and through a hairpin bend followed by a steady descent as our route curves to the northwest. Gradually the forest opens up and we can see that we are some way below our outward route in this great forest filled bowl (115M). We go gently downhill to swing into another valley where a pretty waterfall, cascading down a black cliff-face, graces the valley's head. Shortly after the waterfall we start ascending gently through tall pines before our route levels out to run along a contour. We come onto a steady downhill into another pocket, marked by rock falls from the cliffs alongside the dirt road. Across the head of the pocket we climb gently, and then moderately to go over a crest where beehives (close) and houses (distant) come into view. Below us are cultivated terraces as we contour around the valley wall, crossing a small stream at the head of one pocket. Eventually a steady climb brings us up onto our original outward route (143M). Our final stage is to retrace our outward route back to where Walk 17 meets the tarmac lane (180M), or to where you have parked your car.

HILLSIDE PICNIC.

If you are looking for a short walk to familiarise yourself with Machico we have just the route for you. Add a bottle of wine to your refreshments and follow the start of Walk 15 up to the blue wall. Here we turn right to stroll along the path, which soon leaves the houses behind. In a couple of minutes you come to quiet meadows overlooking Machico town and the beach; just the place for a relaxed picnic on this elevated vantage point.

Glossary

Be aware that the local dialect may be used in place of normal Portuguese for some signs.

achada - plateau
baia - bay
baixo/a - shallow, low
balcões - balconies
boca - mouth, entrance, pass(geo)
brava - wild
cabo - cape(geo)
calheta - small river, stream
caminho - road, pathway
campo - countryside, field, plain
caniço - reed
choupana - shack, cottage
correios - post office
cova - cave
cruz - cross
curral - enclosure, animal pen
encumeada - peak
fajã - landslip
fonte - fountain, spring, source
jardim - garden
levada - man-made irrigation system, watercourses
lombada - ridge
miradouro - viewing point
monte - hill
palheiro - thatched dwelling
paragem - bus stop
pico - peak
portela - doorway
porto - port
quebrada - steep incline
quinta - country estate, farm
ribeira - river
risco - risk, danger
serra - mountain range
vale - valley

Index

Geographical and place names shown on the 1:25000 scale 'OS' maps in Part 1 of this guide, and in the text, appear on these pages.

A
Amparo 3
B
Babosas 14, 16, 18
Boca do Risco 37, 38
C
Camacha 20, 22, 24, 27
Caniçal 30, 31, 32, 33, 34, 35, 37
Caniço 27
Choupana 18, 19, 21
Cova Grande 33
D
Desertas Islands 31
F
Foguete 25
Fonte de Vemelhe 39
Funchal 2, 4, 10, 12, 14, 16, 19, 20, 25, 31
L
Larano 38, 40
Levada da Serra 19, 20, 21, 22
Levada do Caniçal 28, 33, 36, 38, 40
Levada do Curral 8, 9, 11
Levada do Pico do Funcho 9
Levada dos Piornas 2, 5, 8, 11
Levada dos Tornos 15, 16, 18
Lombada 5
Lombo da Quinta 19
M
Machico 28, 29, 30, 33, 35, 36, 37, 39, 41, 42
Maroços 28, 29, 39, 40
Miradouro da Portela 39
Monte 12, 13, 14, 16, 27
P
Pico do Facho 30, 31, 33
Poiso 19
Portela 39
Porto da Cruz 39
Porto Santo 31
Q
Quebradas 2, 4, 11

R
Ribeira da Noia 29
Ribeira das Cales 29
Ribeira de Machico 40
Ribeira do João Gomes 15, 17
Ribeira Grande 29
Ribeira Seca 29, 36, 37, 38
Rochao 24
Romeiros 15, 16, 17, 18, 21
S
Santa Quintera 6, 9
Socorridos Valley 5, 6, 8
T
Terreiro da Luta 12
V
Vale do Paraiso 19, 22